WHEN THE BODY

Your Powerful

To The Point

Book

When the body speaks

by

Edie O'Reilly

WHEN THE BODY SPEAKS

Published by **To The Point**

Next Stage Communications

A Subsidiary of Next Stage Speaking

Copyright © 2019 Edie O'Reilly

All rights reserved. No part of this book may be reproduced or transmitted in any form or by any means, electronic or mechanical, including photocopying, recording or by any information storage an retrieval system, without the written permission of the publisher, except for including of brief quotations in a review.

Next Stage Communications

3638 Tioga Way

Las Vegas, NV 89169

(702) 682-8431

ISBN: 978-1-7338602-0-8

WHEN THE BODY SPEAKS

I dedicate this book to my son Conor. Without him, I wouldn't be the woman I am today. Thank you, Conor for choosing me as your mother.

WHEN THE BODY SPEAKS

Contents

Introduction/Our Agreement 6

3 Steps to Happiness..14

Our Bodies 18

Higher Self...27

Understanding Emotions 34

Head, Heart and Solar Plexus (Gut) 52

Your Solar Plexus 63

Contrast 75

Efforting/Resistance VS. Allowing....................86

Meditation 95

What you Eat, Smell, Touch, Hear and See....104

Feeling Good 115

Beliefs 127

Shifting Language..135

Inspired Action..147

Receiving/Expecting......................................155

In Conclusion...163

About the Author..169

Introduction/Our Agreement

You are amazing!! Your potential is limitless, and your ability is beyond all boundaries!! You were meant to have an amazing life, and everything you need to connect with the amazingness that is you is within you right now. Not one of you were given less than the other no matter what it looks like. The knowledge to have an amazing life is held inside your body and can be released and realized by you at any time.

My whole life has been an ongoing journey of discovery and remembering who I am, and I have worn many hats in my lifetime, as I'm sure you have. One of the hats I wear that has helped me remember many of my hidden gifts, is that of being a parent to my third son, Conor. Conor was born with other abilities, what some would call disabilities, but what I have learned is a wonderful blessing.

Life unfolded for me in a significant way after Conor's birth, but before I get into that let me explain what I had been doing up until he came along.

Before Conor was born, I had been a Clinical Ayurvedic Specialist, coaching clients to be their healthiest by using food as medicine, body treatments and bringing awareness of how your body can heal itself. I was also a yoga instructor and meditation teacher. I was an example of everything I taught others and considered myself to be healthy, grounded and of stable mind. I had been introduced to the idea that we create our own happiness while I lived in an Ashram, but, honestly, I didn't fully understand *how*.

It was with Conor's birth, due to timing and past life (in this lifetime) experiences, that I was led to my most introspective, knowledge increasing time. Throughout this book, I use my life experiences as examples of what I'm trying to convey. Many of the concepts I share with you will have been unveiled to me throughout my entire life, but perhaps not as consciously interpreted as they are now. Through this journey of my life I have realized that even when we think we know a concept, there is perhaps layers of it that aren't revealed or realized at the time of conscious understanding. Once the concept is incorporated into real life, then we grasp and understand it in a deeper way.

I now know how **we entirely create everything that happens to us**, especially happiness, and that is what I wish for you to receive from my book. When the body speaks to you and through you, life makes sense and you realize that you were being guided all along in a tangible, physical way.

It is my hope that with understanding this one foundational concept that you too will fully grasp how everything in your life is created and you can then live the most amazing, happy life.

***

Before we get started, I want to lay a foundation of what my general beliefs are throughout this book.

First, for you to understand anything of what I am sharing with you, there must be an understanding that there is something else that is guiding or overseeing the process of what we call life.

My understanding of what I am referring to above is this; you must have the idea that you are a physical being as well as a spiritual being all at the same time. Most believe we were first spirit, and then we took a human body and now we are physical, this is not fully true. **Both exist at the same time.** I'll explain more about what I mean in a later chapter.

Second, I will be using the term Higher Self and Creator for what others may call Source/Universe or God. I personally am not using the word 'God' because I feel it really limits the all-encompassing energy that is within everything and everybody, quite literally. However, you may substitute 'God' if that is the terminology you connect with most.

Thirdly, let this process take you where you are being led to go. Allow the process to open the possibilities in your mind, because most times change occurs subtly.

By using these concepts/processes, you will have a good understanding of the fantastic life you have been given to live and your role on this planet based on your connection with your Higher Self.

****

If we can agree on the above, then let's get started. **Consciously being aware that you are connecting with your Higher Self through your physical body is what leads to happiness and fulfillment in life.** You can find your life's purpose, you can be happier in general, and you can create the life you want with more intention than ever before. If this is new for you, then you are in for an amazing discovery/unfolding. If you have heard or know these concepts, then I hope you enjoy the journey I have laid out for you.

--Edie O'Reilly

3 Steps to Happiness

Throughout this book you will be guided to understanding your own power and how you create your own happiness in life. The concept of creating happiness is taught throughout almost every Eastern philosophy and though I studied the philosophy while living in an ashram, the understanding on a personal level fully came to fruition once Conor was born.

The 3 Steps are:

1) Feel your emotions in your body.
2) Consciously choose to feel better.
3) Take inspired action.

WHEN THE BODY SPEAKS

Using these 3 steps will not only transform your life but will allow you to understand fully how *you are* creating your own happiness.

"Everything in life is vibration"

-*Albert Einstein*

Step 1:
Feel your emotions in your body

Our Bodies

Scientists from the National Research Nuclear University and collaborators have used a highly sensitive laser device to register infrasonic vibrations in the human body. In fact, you can find numerous studies about the frequency and vibration of the body.

The human body vibrates and responds to vibrations. And every emotion has a vibration. The lower the emotion, the lower the vibration.

Some of us already feel each other, consciously or unconsciously. If you don't think you can, don't worry, you can train yourself to feel the vibrations of people and objects.

Everything on this planet vibrates even the earth herself, and each vibration holds a frequency[1].

Objects, as well as thoughts, hold vibrations and frequencies. When you have a feeling about someone either you like them or dislike them, you are responding to their frequency. We feel frequencies through our solar plexus like a radio tuner. And you tune your radio (solar plexus) with your thoughts. I will talk more about your solar plexus in a later chapter.

[1] The number of **vibrations** or oscillations made in one second is called the **frequency of vibration.**

WHEN THE BODY SPEAKS

Have you ever noticed that when you don't feel good, everything that could go wrong does? And conversely, when you are in a great mood everything that could go right, goes right?

This is because you are tuned to a frequency (good or bad, positive or negative) and you attract more of whatever that frequency is; in other words, you are attracting more negativity or more positivity depending on what frequency you are on. Remember, you are always tuned to a frequency.

You have complete control over your tuning; however, most of us let our life circumstances dictate how we feel at any given time.

Consequently, we don't control our frequencies. I would like you to know that **your body was made for you to vibrate on purpose.**

Just like you have control over the radio in your vehicle so you can tune to the channel that is nice to hear, you can also tune your body (by using your emotions) into attracting more of what is nice for you to experience.

"If you want to find the secrets of the universe, think in terms of energy, frequency and vibration."
*– **Nikola Tesla***

When you see the world through vibration and frequency you realize that the connections you have with each person is not visible with the eye but visible through how you feel. That is why when you hear that everyone and everything is connected it is hard to know *how* because it's not something you can see. **We are all connected through our emotions** (frequency/vibration).

Most of us don't understand the importance of our emotions or that we can feel them with our physical body. Through the awareness of what thought you are having at any given time you can understand the vibration you are on. You can then change what is happening in your life to what you want to be attracting by changing how you feel. I will explain more about your emotions in a later chapter.

For now, what I would like you to understand is the interconnectedness of your thoughts, feelings/emotions, and vibration. They, combined, create what you experience.

WHEN THE BODY SPEAKS

Question:

What frequency (vibration/emotion) are you tuned in to most of the time?

WHEN THE BODY SPEAKS

Notes:

"Every man is a divinity in disguise, a god playing the fool."

— ***Ralph Waldo Emerson***

WHEN THE BODY SPEAKS

Higher Self

Your Higher Self is a much bigger part of you that is non-physical. **Your Higher Self has the bigger view and connects with you through the language/emotion of love, contentment and satisfaction.** When you aren't feeling the higher emotions that make you feel good you are not picking up clearly the messages from your Higher Self.

Your Higher Self is constantly sending you guidance. But when you are feeling numb, sad, grief or any feeling that is not the feeling of satisfaction, love or contentment then you are not clearly picking up the guidance that is given to you.

Throughout my own life I have realized that life experiences are not happening **to** me, they are happening **for** me. It is all in how you look at what is happening. I have literally transformed situations by feeling as if it were happening *for* me. Once I did that, I then understood *why* it was happening.

You can feel the difference in your body. When I say life is happening **to** me, I feel yucky in my gut or solar plexus area. When I say life is happening **for** me, I get a light feeling and it feels better.

WHEN THE BODY SPEAKS

I use this technique when I hear anything new. I *feel* its truth in my gut to see if it is true for me. If I get that light feeling in my gut, I know it is true for me and I also know it is what my Higher Self knows to be true.

When I refer to your Higher Self in this book, I mean the emotion or feelings of love, contentment and satisfaction. That is the language of your Higher Self and it is through that language that you can communicate.

Furthermore, it is my strong belief that we were created to be empowered. We were made to have guidance and to experience life in an energetic, inspired and empowered way. I also feel to be true that there is nothing out there trying to get me or trying to take away from my life. I have control over all aspects. These are my truths that I feel in my gut.

The power is within me to create my own happiness. By understanding my Higher Self and understanding that feeling my Higher Self requires me to essentially feel good first, I can align with and feel my guidance and truth. And so can you.

WHEN THE BODY SPEAKS

Questions:

Try *feeling* your body when you think about the different beliefs you currently have.

Are there any beliefs that make your gut feel yucky? If there is, it simply means that your Higher Self does not hold that belief with you.

If there are beliefs that feel good, then know that you are in alignment with your Higher Self and that belief currently serves you or benefits you in some way right now.

Notes:

"When dealing with people, remember you are not dealing with creatures of logic, but with creatures of emotion."

-**Dale Carnegie**

Understanding Emotions

We are emotional beings. Every single one of us was given emotions.

Have you ever asked yourself Why?

What if the answer was- **We have emotions to be used as a guidance system to be felt in our body!!**

Your emotions are here to guide you through life! They are an internal, hard-wired, connection to your Higher Self/Source. They give you constant physical feedback letting you know if the thought you are thinking is leading you on the path that your Higher Self knows to be true and feels like love and contentment, or away from it.

It is important to know what emotions are on the lower vibrational scale and which ones are on the higher end. But **what's most important is how the emotion *feels* in the body.** You could be feeling an emotion on the lower end of the scale but feel better by feeling another negative emotion. Here's an example; say you were feeling depressed and you were tired of always feeling depressed and so you wanted to feel better and the next emotion you felt was anger. That was a step from where you were and so you started feeling better. **It's most important to know how you are feeling in relation to what emotion/thought you are having**. Because when you know how you are feeling *physically*, then you can change the thought and feel the release in the body.

Here are some examples of emotions/feelings that make your body feel bad:

Depressed, Sad, Angry, Frustrated, Hurt, Pessimistic, Doubtful, Grief, Agitated, Annoyed, Irritated, Critical, Resentful, Bitter, Crushed, Mad, Fed up

WHEN THE BODY SPEAKS

These are some examples of emotions/feelings that allow your body to feel good:

Empowered, Powerful, Bold, Unique, Ambitious, Determined, Inspired, Secure, Confident, Focused, Courageous, Charmed, Joyful, Loving, Optimistic, Glad, Delighted

***

When my third son Conor came into this world, he was born with serious health conditions. His little lungs wouldn't absorb oxygen, and his heart had a defect that required him to be on a ventilator and isolated so that I could not touch him. Day in and day out I sat at his bedside and was his voice. I felt like a solder that oversaw protecting his little body. "Doctor tell me why you are doing that," I constantly questioned.

"Nurse, does he really need this?" I found myself repeating.

I challenged everyone that came within a foot of his body and I questioned why and if it was necessary. All the while my questioning felt like I was trying to push against a solid wall that wasn't budging, yet I continued pushing.

For five months I went to and from the Neonatal Intensive Care Unit. For those five months it was touch and go with Conor's life. Because I wasn't consciously aware of what I was doing I didn't know how to stop myself from reacting emotionally to the situation.

I felt like someone had pushed the pause button on my life. The doctors didn't give Conor much hope and I had conversations with them about taking him off life support and letting him go. I was living my worst nightmare and was being pulled down an emotional rabbit hole and reacting to everything.

Just when things couldn't get any worse, after 5 months, Conor contracted meningitis. I was sure there was no way he could make it through this and in fact, I was once again being asked about letting him go. At that moment I could feel my body and how all the negativity was physically making me sick, drained and lethargic.

I don't know if it was the overwhelm of negative emotions that was too much for me to take in, but, at that moment, I remembered my background and training in meditation. I also remembered the concept first introduced to me while living in an Ashram, *you create your own happiness.*

It was as if I had been reminded of an old healing technique that I had abandoned. With the memory came a strong impulse to feel better. That impulse coursed through me and two little questions popped into my head that changed everything, "Edie, what if this was happening *for* you?" and "What if there are blessings here that you aren't seeing?"

At that moment I let go….I let go of the resistance…..I let go of the need to keep Conor alive….I let go.

Once I let go, a feeling of relief rushed over me and through my body, and I felt light and hopeful and I knew that everything was perfect no matter what it looked like. I was ok with however Conors life was going to turn out, and I felt good in the release of the fight for the first time since my nightmare began five months ago.

That night I left the Neonatal Intensive Care Unit a different woman. I was no longer stuck in a rabbit hole, but I found myself on the outside looking at the situation with clarity and knowing that life will be as it is and it's all working out as it should. You see, I let go of the need to try to control a situation, and I allowed what needed to happen without my resistance, to happen. Instead of pushing on the solid wall it was as if I finally realized that I could walk around it and therefore move forward. The resistance left my body and I felt the lightness of once again being aligned with my Higher Self.

The next morning, I arrived at the hospital, and Conor was doing better, and from that day on he continued to improve. For the next three months Conor grew in strength while the nurses and doctors weaned him off his medications until the day came when he finally came home.

What I realized:

In my darkest hours, I was able to be a witness to one of our amazing gifts, and that is the gift of our emotions.

It was that night that I realized the power of my feelings/emotions and how I was affecting the situation. I also want to add here that everyone, including brand new babies, have their own journeys. I may have been influencing how *long* Conor was in the hospital, but whether he lived or died was his journey.

By releasing my control/resistance and allowing myself to *feel* better I became aware of how I was influencing the situation. I also saw the situation differently and a broader awareness came into my consciousness and I understood the everything was perfect.

We all have times when we want something to happen so badly that we feel awful in the process of trying to get it to happen. **In feeling bad, we are repelling what we want to happen and attracting what we don't want.** Remember that your emotions are a powerful tool that at any moment lets you know how connected you are to your Higher Self or not. Bad feelings in your body mean you are disconnected while feeling good means you are right on track.

My bad feelings were telling me that my thoughts weren't in alignment with what my Higher Self knew about the situation. When I finally released the control, I fell into alignment and therefore I felt better and Conor improved.

***

Always remember that even though you may be aware of a new learning/remembering lesson, old patterns have the upper hand in life and we generally slip back into them until we are more stable and solid in our knowledge.

I found myself, after Conor came home, back down the rabbit hole of my emotions and reacting to almost everything in a very negative way. Once he came home, I felt it was up to me to keep him alive. I took that role very seriously. I isolated myself, for the most part, because I didn't want to miss the signs if Conor needed me. Whatever the reason, the full remembering and realization of that day in the hospital did not solidify within me until, after 4 years of isolation, I realized that I was not living, nor was I happy. In hindsight I would have called myself depressed. When I awoke this time, to the awareness that my body was all bunched up and I didn't 'feel' good about life, I realized what I had done in the hospital and applied that same knowledge to my current situation and once again, everything changed.

Just know that when you start to remember your own power, it may feel like you slip back into old patterns, but you never do. Instead you have another moment where you can solidify what you previously remembered but didn't fully understand or internalize. You essentially were given another opportunity to fully grasp what you already knew.

WHEN THE BODY SPEAKS

Question:

Is there anything going on right now or in the past that feels/felt bad?

WHEN THE BODY SPEAKS

Notes:

WHEN THE BODY SPEAKS

"The way to your spirit is through your body."
— **Ashley Asti**

WHEN THE BODY SPEAKS

Head, Heart and Solar Plexus (Gut)

Consciousness or our Higher Self speaks through our body (head, heart and gut). Let's talk about the differences between them and how and when you can use each to guide you on your life's journey.

We are always receiving guidance from our Higher Self and most of the time it will be a thought or an impulse that comes into your head. However, if you're not feeling satisfied, connected or in the flow of life (which feels really good) your thoughts are not coming from your Higher Self. It is good to get into a routine of asking yourself, "How am I feeling?",

WHEN THE BODY SPEAKS

before acting upon a thought. If you feel good, then go through with the thought or impulse. If you don't feel good, then know that if you act upon the thought you could get mixed results.

In general, your head is where impulses will come when you are in alignment with your Higher Self. When you aren't in alignment your head can lead you down a negative road and all sorts of problems can arise. The connection between your head and your feelings/emotions is what's going to help you understand if you are being guided by your Higher Self or not.

If you are guided by your head while not in alignment, you will make plans, set goals and work hard to meet them. Your head wants to figure everything out on its own. It often over thinks things and the results come with lots of hard work and effort. This is not to say you can't reach goals using your head, on the contrary, you can. But at what expense? Here are some indicators that you are mostly being lead by your head not in alignment:

- Constantly tired and drained
- Headaches
- Hypersensitive
- Anxiety
- Depression
- OCD

- High Blood Pressure
- Other heart-related issues
- Cannot do anything without at first figuring it out

These are just some of the indicators. Most people have been trained to believe that the mind is the only way to get something accomplished.

Unless you are in alignment and feel satisfied and positive, your head will not know the correct route to lead you to your happiness. **You must first be happy to be guided to more happiness.**

***

WHEN THE BODY SPEAKS

Moving on down the body, let's talk about the heart. I've heard people say that we should let our heart lead the way, and I've heard others say don't let your heart lead the way. So, which is it? In my opinion, the heart is your center for love. Love is an emotion and love is good, but love can get too involved emotionally.

However, when love is in alignment with your Higher Self, meaning you feel satisfied and positive and you get an impulse from your heart to do something it will be as if magic happened.

Love is all we are, essentially, and is what connects us to each other (the Creators energy is that of complete, unconditional love). The heart works well for empowering things, for putting intention and for letting yourself feel and be inspired creatively. But I, personally, don't let my heart lead me. I find that those led by the heart experience:

- Strong emotions
- Get hurt easily
- Base decisions on how they feel (good or bad)
- Are controlled by their empathy

While there isn't a strong reason why you shouldn't let your heart guide you, just be aware that the heart can be overly emotional. Being overly emotional also leads to unwanted situations. **We want our emotions only to be an indicator if we are in alignment with our Higher Self or not.**

However, being inspired by the heart can lead to some amazing creations when used by anyone wanting to create artistically, and that is when I would allow my heart to be my guide.

***

And finally, the solar plexus, located in the belly region and often referred to as the gut. This is where you can ask any question and bring any subject and receive an emotion/vibrational response. The emotion will indicate if you are in alignment with your Higher Self, or not. I get into more details about this region in the next chapter but for now remember, good emotions or rather, emotions that feel good indicate you are in alignment with what your Higher Self knows about you. Feeling bad only means you are thinking a thought that isn't true and therefore isn't aligned with what your Higher Self knows about you. The stronger the negative emotion is that you feel, the further away you are from what is true.

WHEN THE BODY SPEAKS

Questions:

What do you use mostly to guide yourself? Head, heart or gut?

Are you open to try using different areas to be inspired to action?

WHEN THE BODY SPEAKS

Notes:

WHEN THE BODY SPEAKS

"You know the truth by the way it feels" - Unknown

WHEN THE BODY SPEAKS

Your Solar Plexus

Your solar plexus is an area of your body located in your belly region. It is where you can *feel* a thought and is often referred to as your gut.

A lot of us let our negative emotions or life circumstances lead our way in life. We are reactive, and if something good happens to us then we are happy, and we feel good, but if something bad happens to us we are not, and we feel bad.

This is not the best way to live your life because **you can't control circumstances, people or events. You can only control your response to them.**

WHEN THE BODY SPEAKS

Let's step back from allowing circumstances and negative emotions to lead the way and instead use your thoughts and emotions to feel your internal guidance system.

Practice feeling your internal guidance system; Ask yourself, "Is there anything going on in my life right now or in the past that feels/felt really bad?" Try and feel that life experience in your solar plexus, or rather, feel your body as you bring up the past memory. This is a negative emotion, and this is what it feels like in your body. Can you feel it?

Now try and think about something you really, really like. I would choose to be with a baby or an animal and again, focus on the solar plexus area (your belly region). How do you feel? This is what a positive emotion feels like in your body.

The link between you and your Higher Self is connected through your emotions and felt mostly in the solar plexus. When you think a thought that doesn't make you feel good you are disconnecting from your Higher Self. **Your Higher Self is pure love and knows your next, best step forward, and when you are thinking thoughts that go against your next, best step, you feel bad.** That's all a negative feeling means.

WHEN THE BODY SPEAKS

Common ways we allow ourselves to disconnect from our Higher Self is when we engage in conversations with others or ourselves that feels yucky. We also disconnect when *we come down to another person's level* to better relate with them. We can't help others when we are down on the floor with them. We only help others when we maintain a positive outlook and bring them up. Not the other way around.

If you find yourself trying to help a friend that is down and you find yourself also feeling bad during or after the interaction then make sure the next time you 'try and help them' you are in a pure positive space and never allow yourself to go lower than where you are. Walk away before that happens.

I also want to shine a light on old stories. Old stories stay current and alive in your now when you repeat them now. **Now is where your power is and the only time that matters.** If you are repeating a story that doesn't feel good, you keep it fresh and current. Let it go or understand the larger lesson behind it so that you can move on. You are helping nobody, especially yourself, if you are stuck in the past repeating a story that doesn't feel good. When you understand <u>why</u> what happened to you happened in the first place, you rewrite your history and change a negative into a positive.

One of the easiest ways to help others is to connect (through getting yourself in a feeling good space) to your Higher Self and see everyone as perfect just as they are. By knowing everyone is perfect you help bring them into their own alignment. If, however, you focus on the problem you are increasing the problem. We aren't here to talk about our problems, because when we do, we increase them.

When you can view life as happening FOR you, problems and concerns take on a whole different message. I know that won't be easy for some to hear, but I promise if you can change the dialog about something that is happening in your life that isn't "good" and **see it as happening FOR you, you will feel the power that you have and the situation will be transformed.**

Anytime you are presented with a problem you will never be able to solve that problem by focusing on it and creating a plan of action to "fix" it. The only way to "fix" a problem is to see the situation as perfect (doesn't mean you have to like the situation), turn to thoughts that make you feel good, release the tension in your solar plexus and allow what needs to unfold. Step away and don't give it any more of your attention. **When we start tuning into our solar plexus/gut when it comes to making decisions, we allow the magic of life to happen.**

Remember when I shared my story about Conor in the hospital? I felt awful and depressed. I was feeling those emotions and only perpetuating the problem because of my strong negative emotion and my fixation on him being sick. Once I let go of trying to make him better, everything changed because I stopped focusing on the problem and instead focused on feeling better. The release in my gut was instant and felt like salve put on a festering wound. **This did not mean I liked the situation,**

but the situation could not have changed unless I let go of the yucky feeling/resistance. I know that the path to change the situation was always being shown to me, but I wasn't seeing it because of all the angst and negative emotions I was feeling.

Questions:

How do you mostly feel every day? If you don't have an overall emotion that you are feeling, then pay attention over the next couple of days to see if you can get an idea of what your dominant emotion is. Your life reflects what your dominant emotion is.

Throughout your day, try and tune into either your head, heart or gut to decide. I would encourage you to use a region you don't regularly use. What were the results?

WHEN THE BODY SPEAKS

Notes:

"You're going to go through tough times - that's life. But I say, 'Nothing happens to you, it happens for you.' See the positive in negative events". -**Joel Osteen**

Contrast

Contrast is when you are faced with a situation that you know you don't want. Let's face it, life happens, and contrast is important because to understand what you want, you must know what you don't want.

Throughout your day you are given opportunities to discover what you want by having contrasting moments. **These moments are not happening to you so you can get lost in how wrong or bad they are, they are there to show you how you prefer life to be.** And by giving them your attention whether you wanted it or not you give them power.

Often, you not only give the contrast your attention, but you also provide it with power by becoming negatively, emotionally involved in what's happening.

When I was in the hospital with my son Conor, I had a contrasting moment that lead into a long stay because I was constantly negative and emotionally ill with how I saw the situation. Had I viewed what happened as what it was, a contrasting moment (I want my son healthy vs. my son sick), then I could have moved faster through the process of releasing the resistance and allowing what needed to happen.

You can release contrasting moments by, instead of thinking about what you don't like or want in any situation, you *think about what you do want*, and *feel* it in your solar plexus. It's important to feel that release in your solar plexus to change the situation.

I have a couple of phrases that I use to help me shift from a negative feeling thought to a positive one. The first phrase I use is, "Everything is always working out for me." Even if I first don't believe it, I act as if. If everything was working out for me allows me to trust that there is a bigger picture that I don't know, and I can let go. Letting go just means I stop trying to figure out why this is happening and instead trust that it is good.

The second phrase I use is, "What if…(I follow the what if with what situation I would like to see even if I don't currently believe it). What if this is perfect as it is? The, what if, let's the wall down that keeps me from seeing a different side of the story.

Both phrases release any resistance I have in my solar plexus and allows the love and therefore what I really want to see happen to flow. I want to make a note here that **I am not changing my thoughts so I can change the situation around me, I am changing my thoughts because I want to feel better.** Isn't that why you want to change the situation in the first place, so you can feel better? **When you feel better first, the situation changes to support you.**

Here is another example of changing how I felt and then the situation changed. Conor is tube fed (he gets most of his nutrition, a blended diet of "regular" food, through a tube that goes directly into his stomach). He has what is called a "button" in his abdomen that the feeding tube attaches to. Because the button is not natural the body will sometimes create tissue around it to try and push the "foreign object" out. The tissue is called granulated tissue. Conor's granulated tissue needed to be removed and I needed to take him in to see his doctor (what I wanted). When I called to make an appointment, I was told that the doctor was booked for the next four months (contrasting moment- what I didn't want). I felt frustrated (negative emotional response), but I didn't hold on to the emotion and booked the next available appointment. I focused on what made me happy-not looking back and talking about how long it will take to get in to see the doctor.

Not even a day later Conors current button broke. We have been having ongoing issues with the buttons breaking and so when I called the company that supplies them, they told me that I had already used up all the buttons we are allowed through insurance and they aren't able to send us a new one for three more months unless we went to see the doctor. At the time I was not happy (another negative emotional response to a contrasting moment), and I reacted to the situation by saying, "Why should I need to take him to see the doctor again when it's because the buttons defected?"

Almost immediately after feeling the uneasy feeling in my solar plexus I said to myself, "Everything is always working out for me," and I let it go. I didn't see it immediately, but the outcome was we got right in to see the doctor because now we had extenuating circumstances that required immediate attention. Consequently, Conor got his granulated tissue removed.

Had I not released the negative feelings/emotions when it came to the appointment, I am sure the button would not have broken. And though, at first, I wasn't happy about it breaking, I quickly understood why it was all happening.

Questions:

What contrasting moments have you felt today?

Is there a big contrasting situation that you continue to give emotion to therefore keeping it in your life?

WHEN THE BODY SPEAKS

Notes:

WHEN THE BODY SPEAKS

"If you knew your potential to feel good, you would ask no one to be different so that you can feel good. You would free yourself of all that cumbersome impossibility of needing to control the world, or control your mate, or control your child. You are the only one who creates your reality. For no one else can think for you, no one else can do it. It is only you, every bit of it you."
— ***Esther Hicks***

Efforting/Resistance VS. Allowing

Effort means just that, trying to make something happen by your action. Most of us have been born to effort our way through life because that was how we were taught by our parents. Effort alone does produce results, but the results are hard, they take time, and you feel drained from the process. The whole terminology around working hard to succeed came from this idea.

Here is what I want you to keep in mind when you think about effort alone; effort creates resistance and resistance creates stress and stress creates disease. It's important to understand this concept of effort alone because it makes results hard to accomplish. This is how people end up stressed and sick.

However, there must be some effort in life to make something happen. But instead of calling it effort I'm going to call it action and inspired action is where you want to be working from. **Inspired action is that impulse that comes to you once you are in a feel-good space and is called allowing.**

I want to talk about the art of allowing. Most of us know how to effort something but allowing is a much harder concept.

Allowing means to see clearly what it is that you want and let go of thinking how and what steps need to happen until you are inspired to do so. Let go of the need to control the process.

Allow the steps to show themselves. I know what you are thinking, "If I don't do something it won't happen." Or, "It will take too long if I just let something happen in its own time." Yes and no. You aren't really doing nothing except letting go of the need to plan and create the steps you think it will take to achieve results. **When you allow through inspired action results happen effortlessly and fast.** There is often no waiting and sometimes you wonder how so much happened so quickly.

I grew up in a very controlling environment. Most of us have. Either one or both of my parents wanted the say in everything that happened and I never learned to allow. I was controlled by being told what to do. Allowing is the opposite of controlling and has a much easier energy about it.

When you want something to happen you:

1. First, have a contrasting moment (not reacting just observing) to know what you don't want you need to know what you do want.

2. You clearly envision, in your mind's eye, what you do want.
3. Feel the emotions in your solar plexus and feel the joy in having/achieving what you want and see it done.
4. Then you let the whole process go. **Don't** try to figure it out. **Don't** write down what steps you think need to happen and what you can do first.
5. Focus on what makes you feel good and happy in life and allow what you envisioned to show the steps to you.

WHEN THE BODY SPEAKS

This is how we create what we want. The key to creating is feeling good.

When, after you envision what you want, you feel inspired to write down action steps, then do so. But always ask yourself, "What am I under the influence of?" Because **inspired action feels fun. It feels good and you want to do it.**

Allowing is an energy that is about feeling your way to your truth. Allowing feels good in your solar plexus. When you are in the energy of allowing you to feel good and inspiration comes.

Questions:

What are you currently trying to make happen based on your effort?

How's that working out for you?

Have you ever allowed something to happen *for* you?

If you haven't, then take some time now to think of something you want (make it something you think would be simple) and think of it having happened then let it go. Don't think about it again in the same way, just know that it is happening for you and that you are allowing it.

WHEN THE BODY SPEAKS

Notes:

"Where there is peace and meditation, there is neither anxiety or doubt"

- *St. Francis de Sales*

Meditation

I can not go any further in this book without bringing up meditation. Meditation is key to knowing and allowing your Higher Self to communicate with you.

Meditation is merely a one-pointed focus. If you don't currently have a meditation practice and/or you have tried it in the past, and it didn't work for you, then I want you to loosen your idea of what you think meditation is and try again. There are many ways to meditate, and none of them are better than the next. The overall purpose is to make sure your mind is focused on one thing.

WHEN THE BODY SPEAKS

If your mind is currently too active to sit still, then do a walking meditation. Walking meditation is done by paying attention to every single step you take. Pay attention to how your step feels in your foot as you place your foot on the floor. Pay attention to where the pressure comes up from your foot and how your foot feels in the shoes or bare on the ground. Become fully aware in the moment. That is meditation.

Another idea is meditating while doing the dishes. This means that all your thoughts are fully engaged in what you are doing. No distractions.

WHEN THE BODY SPEAKS

You can, of course, engage in a traditional meditation practice which is about finding a quiet place every day, at the same time, and focus on a single thought/sound/breath. Whatever you choose, make it easy and don't try too hard. This is not a chore to torture you with, but **a tool to connect you with your Higher Self and allow you to receive messages that are coming to you every day, all day.**

If you already connect easy and you have a different way to do that, then great! No need to meditate. But most of us do not have that connection as open and flowing as we could.

WHEN THE BODY SPEAKS

Meditation is so crucial in feeling your connection because sometimes, especially when people are just learning, it is very subtle and hard to feel your body. Through meditation, you learn to take a break from the ramblings of the mind.

There are many benefits to meditation. As you meditate more often, you will notice that you have increased energy throughout the day; like charging your batteries. You aren't as involved in arguments, and you're able to see the other's viewpoint easier. You also tend to be quieter throughout your day. This could be a change for those that engage in a lot of idle talk and gossip.

When and if you do find yourself in a disagreement you don't allow it to get out of control. **Meditation makes everything less dramatic**, and therefore you tend to stay out of the emotional rabbit hole rather than get lost in it.

I started meditating about 18 years ago. I had periods when I did it very little and times when I did it every day, twice a day. I know myself how it feels to be under the influence of meditation. I can say that all that I mentioned above is so true once you start meditating regularly. You will find yourself in a much lighter, happier mindset and one that will allow you to deal with more significant issues without getting lost. It's mental health, naturally.

WHEN THE BODY SPEAKS

Questions:

Do you currently meditate?

If no, what stops you?

WHEN THE BODY SPEAKS

Notes:

WHEN THE BODY SPEAKS

"Food for the body is not enough. There must be food for the soul"

— **Dorothy Day**

WHEN THE BODY SPEAKS

What you Eat, Smell, Touch, Hear and See

Like meditation, it's important to know that what you 'do' with your body affects your ability to 'feel' what's going on in your body especially in the beginning. Essentially, the cleaner the vessel, the easier to transmit and connect with your Higher Self.

Food is how you feed your physical body through your five senses: your eyes, mouth, ears, nose, and sense of touch. All the senses feed your body and can hinder or heighten your connection to your Higher Self (remember the Higher Self is satisfaction, love and flow of life).

I don't want to make a big deal about what you eat, but what you eat is one of the ways you block your connection because what you eat contributes to the overall health of your body as well as your emotions.

To increase the best emotions within you and the best health it's always better to eat home cooked meals made from organic, fresh foods. Staying clear of processed (boxed, precooked), canned, frozen (in most cases) and old foods (leftovers more than 2 days old). Cleaner food will aid the body in being clear as well as help your overall emotional state.

If you are in a habit of eating foods that are not good for you and the thought of eating 'healthy' foods creates negative emotion within you then it's best you come at it from a different angle. This is where working with a coach can help. Sometimes changes that are good for us makes us feel overwhelmed and worked up. You don't have to make the changes on your own and getting help is going to be your best way to success. Keep in mind that the end goal is to be in control of your emotions and to be happy.

Other ways you hinder your body's ability to connect is through stimulants such as coffee, black tea, and sugar or drugs, alcohol, and tobacco. It's not that you can't connect if you do the above things, in fact, you will never completely lose your connection, EVER (because it is you), but you won't have control over your connection if your body isn't clear. All the above foods and substances hinder your bodies connection clarity.

Also, bring your awareness to what you feed yourself through television, videos, social media and movies. These are distractions in life that lead you down the road of emotional rollercoastering and hinder you from feeling and knowing your connection to your Higher Self.

WHEN THE BODY SPEAKS

There was a time in my life when I lived in an ashram for a couple of years. An ashram is like a monastery (at least the one I was in) where we had daily routines and ritual. We meditated twice a day, Yoga/asana class twice a day and we ate an organic vegetarian diet twice a day. My body felt clean and very efficient, and I was able to feel every little emotion that flowed through me. There were minimal distractions. No television, no radios or newspapers and being disconnected from the outside world felt fresh and healing. It was a great time to really discover myself and my tendencies. I really got to know my body and how the senses can be used to distract us from knowing who we are.

I strongly encourage you to take some time to limit your distractions and/or clean up what you are ingesting. You will notice your feelings/emotions, and from there you can control your thoughts to lift yourself up and connect to your Higher Self.

Having said all that, once you are guided by your Higher Self and your connection is flowing through you every day, all day, you could eat anything because, at that time, you realize that everything holds divine energy in it. You will unconsciously be repulsed by things that don't feel good in your body so you will make decisions based on how good it makes you feel or not.

WHEN THE BODY SPEAKS

Questions:

How are you being distracted through your senses?

What is your biggest distraction?

Notes:

WHEN THE BODY SPEAKS

"Happiness is not something ready made. It comes from your own actions."

— **Dalai Lama**

Step 2:
Choose to Feel Better

Feeling Good

There is nothing more important in life except that you feel good. **Your number one reason for being on this planet is to enjoy the unfolding of you and to feel good in the process.** I can't place enough emphasis on the importance of this.

You give yourself many reasons why you don't feel good. You could physically have a problem, so you don't feel good, or you could be disconnected from your emotions and how they feel in your body and therefore not feel right. You could also have a trauma in your life that justifies why you don't feel good. If you find yourself not feeling well most of the time, then it's time for a change.

Every day I find ways to keep myself inspired and feeling good because I know how important it is to stay feeling good. Here are some examples that I have used to feel good:

- Meditate
- Take a nap
- Listen/read a book that inspires me
- Listen to a speaker that inspires me
- Listen to music that inspires me (being careful of lyrics and making sure they are uplifting)

- Remind myself every day of the thousands of blessing I have/am just by being alive
- Bringing myself into the now moment and knowing that is where my power is
- Reminding myself of all that I appreciate in my world
- Repeat the phrase 'I am' and add whatever you are looking at. For example, 'I am that flower", 'I am the trees', 'I am Sally' (add the name of someone that inspires you)
- Repeating the phrase, 'Everything is always working out for me.'

Whenever I do any of the above, I do it to put myself in a state that is in alignment with my Higher Self, and I know when I'm there by how I feel. When **you feel and witness the world through love, everything feels and is good.** Here are some indicators when you are aligned:

- You are excited about your future
- You know that everything is always working out for you
- You have a smile on your face, and you can't wait to do the next thing
- There is an expectation about what will happen next, and you cannot wait to see what's around the corner
- There is a lightness about you, and you see others

responding to you in a very positive way
- You are attracting everything you need to grow
- You get an inspired action to do what you need to further your dreams
- Your life unfolds in such a way that it feels magical and you are in awe

I could keep going on because the feeling of being aligned is so wonderful that you will know when you are there. And once you get there, you know that there are no mistakes in this world, and everything is exactly as it should be.

When I lived in the ashram, I had a beautiful moment that I had not been able to explain until I understood the power of being in alignment with my Higher Self and therefore unconditional love.

I had been assigned the duty of cleaning the Durga Temple. So every day I took my 3-month-old baby and walked the ½ mile to the Durga temple all the while repeating to myself, 'I am the oak tree', 'I am the grass blowing in the wind', 'I am the water in the pond', and every time I claimed to be one of these objects I imagined, within myself, how it must feel to actually be that.

I continued the process, and once I got to the temple, I sang songs that helped me stay in a positive, light mood while I cleaned the temple. Once finished I started walking back on the same route repeating the same, 'I am the grass' and felt what that might be like and on I went until I looked over at a huge fallen tree and repeated, 'I am that fallen tree.' Suddenly, my vision changed. Everything blurred just a little, and I saw colors I had never seen before. Everything around me shimmered and danced with colors and movement that was so beautiful and so beyond words it took my breath away. I stood there, with my mouth open and my eyes wide trying to take it all in. I'm not sure how much time went by before my baby moved in the front pack, and I popped out. I then realized that I probably did not breath during that whole time as I found myself taking in large amounts of air. My legs were shaking as I looked for something to sit down on. I felt so light and happy inside with what I had just viewed. I instantly wanted to go back but didn't grasp how I had gotten there in the first place so was finding it hard to repeat the process.

What I realize now is that I had put myself in perfect alignment with viewing the world through the eyes of unconditional love. You see, we are all one. Everything is interconnected. The connecting factor is love itself living within each and every*thing* on this planet (no exception). Our Higher Self is *felt* by the body through the feelings of unconditional love, satisfaction and contentment.

I had connected to that which unites us all by playing the game 'I am' and imagining how it feels to be each and everything I said I was without judgement. This concretely showed me that I was never alone and that my guidance system is hard-wired to my Higher Self so I always know if I am aligned with it or not. I know it through how I feel; my positive emotions.

Questions:

What do you now do to feel good in the day?

Do you know how important feeling good is?

WHEN THE BODY SPEAKS

Notes:

WHEN THE BODY SPEAKS

"The only limits you have are the limits you believe"

-*Wayne Dyer*

Beliefs

You cannot see or believe what is beyond your beliefs. Your beliefs are the foundation of your life. Your beliefs lead you through life and can continue to unfold you or hold you right where you are. It's your choice. You were given free will to go and find what feels right and true for you. And, just because you believe something does not mean it is right for everyone.

When I sat down to write this book, I sat down to write down my beliefs. These are my beliefs that I have discovered through living life and what has brought me to a deeper understanding and knowledge about my life.

My beliefs have changed over time, and what I once believed to be true I may not believe any longer. But I have allowed myself to unfold and remember as I go through life by keeping my mind open to situations and understandings.

I use my solar plexus to guide me towards what I know is my best life because my connection to my Higher Self is through my solar plexus. And I feel my truth, and therefore my truth is my belief. But I also know that you may not have the same truths. And that is ok. We are all on our own journey, and every journey is of value to the whole.

I did not always use my solar plexus to guide me through life. In the past, I would tune in to what felt right in my gut on occasion, but I mostly used my head. What I found, when I used my head, was that I would worry about life and I found myself depressed and feeling hopeless. I only allowed myself to be led by my gut when I was in a good mood. I thought I couldn't feel my gut when I was in a bad mood. Now I know that feeling bad in my solar plexus was my gut alerting me that I wasn't aligned with my Higher Self.

WHEN THE BODY SPEAKS

My knowledge/beliefs have been an evolution. An unfolding of remembering who I am and what this amazing body can do.

That is why it is so important to tune into your Higher Self. Your Higher Self will never miss guide you. So, when you read my beliefs in this book and if you feel a ting of not knowing in your solar plexus (not your head) then let the idea or concept pass for now and come back to it later. **Truth unfolds as we can understand it and the truth is felt in the body.**

This book may challenge some or many of your beliefs which only means that you haven't heard the concept or idea before. Usually, it takes time to settle with a new idea or listen to it more than once before considering it as a belief.

Questions:

Have any of the ideas in this book, so far, challenged any of your current beliefs?

If so, how are you feeling about these new ideas?

WHEN THE BODY SPEAKS

Notes:

"Be mindful of your self talk. It's a conversation with the Universe."

– David James Lees

Shifting Language

Changing how you talk about yourself and others will improve your connection with your Higher Self. You see, your body was perfect in the beginning and can still be perfect if you get out of the way and allow it to fall back into that balance. It's your internal dialog that keeps you open or not.

Here is an exercise that will help you to feel where you are at with the language you use towards yourself. I want you to stand in front of a mirror and say the following to yourself:

- I am worth it!
- I am amazing!

- I am powerful!
- My body is strong and healthy!

How did that feel in your body? If it didn't feel true or it felt uncomfortable, then keep repeating until you know, without a doubt, that you are all of the above and more. How you feel about those words is an indicator if you believe about yourself the same as your Higher Self. The worse you felt, the farther away from what your Higher Self feels and knows about you.

The language you use inside your head is the key to knowing yourself. If you don't love yourself or if you think that you're not worth anything then you won't be able to connect to your Higher Self.

Another way to check in with your belief in self-empowering words is how you think and feel about others. **You see in other people what you think and feel about yourself**. If you find yourself being critical of others, then that says you are critical of yourself. Your beliefs and emotions towards others are a mirror reflection of the internal dialog that goes on in your head about yourself.

Use words of love about yourself and others. When you think harshly of others, you are projecting how you really feel about yourself so be aware of what you are putting out there. Awareness is key to everything because if you aren't aware you can't change.

Imagine if you started saying to yourself, "Everything is always working out for me." Or "Life is happening for me, not to me." These are sayings that can change your mindset in a moment of not feeling well.

Once I become aware that I'm not feeling good in my body, I check to find out what I am saying inside my head. I don't know how many times a day I remind myself that everything is always working out for me. In the beginning, I didn't really believe it and I didn't feel that shift in my body. Now I know that it is true and every time I use either of those phrases, I feel the physical release in my gut.

It's so much easier to see the blessings in life when you look at life as happening <u>for you</u>, rather than against you. Your perception of every situation is what makes it good or bad. The situation itself is neither. We give it power or not.

I want to talk a little more about perception. Perception is based on our beliefs, and it would serve you well to challenge your beliefs, daily.

Having Conor has helped challenge many of my beliefs and

perceptions. I know that he is perfect even though he has a trach, is on oxygen 24/7, has a feeding tube, cannot walk or talk and has little control over his motor skills. I didn't really have a perception about others similar to Conor before he came along but having him born to me has opened my eyes to the language other people use and how people, in general, view his life.

As a society, we tend to put a value on others by how much they contribute to society mostly by what they do (work). But value should be given to you because you live not because you do x, y, and z. **You are valued because you are alive.** Every one of us is connected to the Higher Self therefore connected to God and if you think you are better because you are a _____(fill in the blank) then you need to learn more. **That child, with all those complications, is as much connected to God as you are.** So let's change how we look at each other because when we do, we will start changing the language we use towards one another.

When children have what most people call a "disability," they are seen as less than in society. If we must call it anything let's call it "other" ability. My Conor is hard-wired to his Higher Self and knows it, whereas you and I must work at remembering these concepts. This whole book is written to remind you of something that Conor will never forget. **Until we learn to see everyone for the beautiful, connected beings that each of us is, we will never fully know ourselves and the power that we've all come here with**. Let's let go of the labels and less than mentality and honor every single one of us on this planet for the amazingness that is all of us!

WHEN THE BODY SPEAKS

Questions:

Do you think you could improve the language you use about yourself and others?

What does your internal dialog sound like? Is it inspiring?

Think of a phrase that you can start using today that will remind you of the perfection of life and you and write it here.

WHEN THE BODY SPEAKS

Notes:

"Emotional intelligence is the ability to sense, understand, and effectively apply the power and acumen of emotions as a source of human energy, information, connection, and influence".

-Robert K. Cooper, PhD

Step 3:
Take Inspired Action

Inspired Action

The inspired action you take depends on the circumstances you are surrounded by.

When my son Conor was in the hospital I did step 1 (became aware of how my thoughts were feeling in my body) and step 2 (made a conscious decision to change how I felt about the situation) but step 3 (inspired action) was a voice inside my head that guided me towards feeling better. Inspired action could be a voice in your head, an impulse that you act upon once you feel better or a conscious action that you take to make the circumstance better. Or, it could be a saying that you repeat to yourself such as, "Everything is always working out for me." **The key to knowing if it is inspired action is to know how you feel. Inspired action makes you feel better.**

Every single step, of the 3 steps, is improving the overall feeling or emotion in your body.

When our van broke down and we didn't have the credit nor the money saved to replace it, I trusted that we would be taken care of.

The very day the van decided it wasn't going to work anymore, my husband received a letter in the mail from a local car dealership that said because of our great history of paying off our van we qualified for a brand-new car. We didn't know how this was going to happen, but we took one step at a time and didn't allow any doubt to come into our minds.

Doubt is the killer of all happiness. When you doubt, you send out the message that it might not happen and then it usually doesn't. If you are going to believe in something, give it your 100% and don't let doubt get in your way.

One of the easiest ways for doubt to come in is to share what you would like to see happen with someone else. Never share your ideas unless you know, without a doubt, that the person you are sharing with will support what you are trying to do.

At the car dealership the down payment and the monthly price were both over what we could comfortably pay, but we didn't put any angst into the process. We trusted and knew that all was working out for us. In fact, I kept saying, "Everything is always working out for me."

We got our brand-new car with no money down and a payment we could comfortably pay.

Remember that while you are going through the 3 Step process, you don't need to know how. Your job is to trust your belief that it will happen without doubting.

Questions:

We all get inspiration. Pay attention to what you have asked for and how you are inspired. Did the inspiration come as an impulse or a voice in your head?

WHEN THE BODY SPEAKS

Notes:

"When you ask it is given- But at some point you have to stop asking and start expecting".

-Abraham Hicks

Receiving/Expecting

According to the Law of Attraction, once you have asked, it is always given. It is our resistance or thoughts that contradict and stop the receiving.

When you put out your desire or wish for something to happen and you allow or expect it to happen, it happens.

When I first understood my 3 steps, I started applying them to my life. The first application was with our living accommodations. Since we had settled in the area, at that time it was five years, I wanted to move. We had been living in a tiny two-bedroom apartment. There were now five of us there in addition to Conor's supplies and equipment. The apartment got small when Conor came home from the hospital. I started feeling frustrated with not having room and I didn't hesitate to share my dislike and negativity for our apartment, until I understood my 3 steps.

Step 1: I became aware of how I was feeling and thinking in relation to the apartment. I felt claustrophobic, stuck and frustrated. I wanted to move immediately!

Step 2: I decided to change how I felt about where we were living and instead stopped giving it any attention at all. When you give attention to something, negative or positive, you give it energy and you get more of it.

Step 3: I took inspired action by visualizing what it would be like to be living in a larger house with plenty of space for all my boys to have their own rooms. I felt the new house and I appreciated and gave love to what it would be like if it were true. And I consciously made the decision to not look back on the apartment in a negative way. I kept focused on my vision. I expected the new house to happen at any time and throughout my days, gave appreciation for it.

Roughly 5 months later we moved into a 4-bedroom house. We now have plenty of space for everyone and everyday I give thanks for where I live.

I have learned to **not put any negative thinking or emotion into what makes me unhappy**. I didn't know how I was going to get into a house, I just focused on the feeling as if we were in the house. I also didn't keep looking around wondering where the new house was because it didn't happen right away. I trusted and had faith in my vision and feelings of a new, bigger house. I put no doubt in *if* we would get the house. Also note that you don't have to keep asking for something that hasn't happened. Simply focus on how good it feels to have received whatever it is you want. **It is the feeling that is attracting.**

This process worked because I focused on feeling good and I sat in expectation that it would happen. It really wasn't about focusing on the house it was about focusing on what felt good and what would continue to make me feel good, happened.

Moments that make us "unhappy" are doing one of two things; 1) They are happening to show us what we don't want or 2) They are happening to set us up for what we have been asking for or longing for all along. That is why it is important to know your feelings in relation to what you are thinking. But remember this, nothing is happening TO you. **Everything is happening FOR you**. Expect the best and know that life is unfolding perfectly no matter what it looks like.

WHEN THE BODY SPEAKS

Questions:

Is there something you are wanting now that you could use the 3 Steps to Happiness on?

Try using the 3 steps and see what happens.

WHEN THE BODY SPEAKS

Notes:

In Conclusion

We all go through times in our lives when we feel more challenged. It is during the times of challenge that we can grow ourselves by not reacting to the situation, but observing, feeling and choosing the course of inspired action that will empower all of those involved.

In order to stay in your happiness, take these steps:

- Ask yourself, "What am I under the influence of, my head, heart or my Higher Self?"
- Be aware of how and where you are feeling in your body.

- Look at the situation and embrace what is happening lightly.
- Allow the lessons of the moment to unfold without strong emotion attached.
- If you do feel strong emotion, loosen up your grip and go lightly.
- Embrace a saying such as, "Everything is always working out for me." Even if you don't believe what you are saying, act as if it were true and feel what that might be like.

This will allow what needs to happen to happen in an unfolding, empowering way.

WHEN THE BODY SPEAKS

Remember, it's all for your higher good.

With that said, you do not have to experience hardships to learn who you are. You do have to know, however, that your bodies emotions are you hard-wired into your Higher Self and therefore hard-wired into divine energy. You can feel your connection and guidance through your body/gut.

You are the most powerful creation ever created. You can live a life of happiness, heal yourself and inspire others. Your emotions are your connection to your Higher Self, and your Higher Self is all knowing and connected to all that is. Once you understand and embrace how amazing you are, you can literally change your life by allowing yourself to be guided with inspired action directed from your Higher Self.

You are here to have fun. You are here to love. You are here to enjoy the unfolding of remembering who you are on this planet. You are amazing, and there is nothing better than you created! Embrace life and know that you are perfect just as you are!

Happiness is the result of living a life on purpose. Remembering the 3 Steps to Happiness is within your power.

WHEN THE BODY SPEAKS

Step 1: Feel your emotions in your body in relation to what you are thinking

Step 2: Choose to feel better

Step 3: Take inspired action

Emotions can get in the way or get you on the way. **-Mavis Mazhura**

Your intellect may be confused, but your emotions will never lie to you. --**Roger Ebert**

The curious paradox is that when I accept myself just as I am, then I can change.
*-**Carl R. Rogers***

About the Author

Edie has over 13 years' experience working with clients and a lifetime of working on herself. Her full awareness of our inner guidance system revealed itself after her third son was born. Her mission and commitment is to empower individuals in understanding their own emotional guidance system to guide them through life. Edie is fiercely committed to guiding individuals who are stuck and frustrated to achieve satisfying, gratifying, and exciting lives. You can find her at www.edieoreilly.com

www.ingramcontent.com/pod-product-compliance
Lightning Source LLC
Chambersburg PA
CBHW071004160426
43193CB00012B/1914